# Sexual Harassment
## What Teens Should Know

Carol Rust Nash

—Issues in Focus—

**ENSLOW PUBLISHERS, INC.**

44 Fadem Road
Box 699
Springfield, N.J. 07081
U.S.A.

P.O. Box 38
Aldershot
Hants GU12 6BP
U.K.

*This book is dedicated to my parents,
Doris Rust and the late Henry Rust.*

**Library of Congress Cataloging-in-Publication Data**

Nash, Carol Rust.
    Sexual harassment : what teens should know / Carol Rust Nash.
        p. cm. — (Issues in focus)
    Includes bibliographical references and index.
    Summary: Defines sexual harassment, discusses who is guilty and
what characterises the victim, and examines the consequences and
what can be done about the situation.
    ISBN 0-89490-735-2
    1. Sexual harassment in education—United States—Juvenile literature
    2. Teenagers—Sexual behavior—United States—Juvenile literature. [1. Sexual
harassment.] I. Title. II. Series: Issues in focus (Hillside, N.J.)
    LC212.82.N37 1996
    370.19'342—dc20                    95-43806
                                            CIP
                                        AC r96

Printed in the United States of America

10 9 8 7 6 5 4 3 2

**Illustration Credits:** David Rose, illustrations, pp. 23, 35, 42, 46, 57, 62, 73, 76, 94; Carol Rust Nash, photography, pp. 9, 16, 37.

**Cover Illustration:** Photo by Jim Whitmer

# Contents

# Acknowledgments

Special thanks go to my children, Brian, David, and Gordon, for their continued love and encouragement; my husband, Raymond, for asking the question; Deborah McKown for editing expertise, support, and friendship; and David Rose for illustrative talent and keen wit.

# 1

# The Invisible Wound

*"I—I cry in the bathroom. I get upset. . . . I cry at home,"* sixth-grader Eve Bruneau said.[1]

♦ ♦ ♦

*"At night, like, when I'm going, trying to go to sleep, I would just start crying,"* fifth-grader Jessica Hasenbank said.[2]

♦ ♦ ♦

*Jonathan Harms was not attentive; he would not follow instructions. He had developed a tic. He was in third grade.*[3]

♦ ♦ ♦

*Tawnya Brawdy, thirteen, suffered from headaches and stomachaches. She made out a will. She decided to whom she would leave her stuffed animals and tapes.*[4]

*"I think high school is something that most kids look forward to—you see movies, read books about high school being the best time—and I'll always remember dark days, coming home, sitting on my bedroom floor sobbing," fifteen-year-old Katy Lyle said.*[5]

What horrible thing do these students have in common? Did they witness a drive-by shooting? Do they belong to a gang? Are they using drugs? The answer is no. They are all victims of sexual harassment.

*"[I]t affected my school life. I went home and cried every day and I hated school. . . . It totally diminished my self-esteem and it robbed two years of my life and I've been trying hard to get that back. I didn't connect that this harassment was hurting me. I didn't even know it was really harassment. Lots of people don't realize that harassment can hurt. And once I realized that harassment was what was making me feel so bad, I started to feel better instantly and realized that I was wrong. And I blamed myself for a long time and I realized that it wasn't my fault that this happened to me," Katy said.*[6]

*"I can't stay here anymore, Mom," eighth-grader Jane Doe said, sobbing, when her mother picked her up from junior high school.[7] She is known as Jane Doe to protect her anonymity during a lawsuit against Petaluma, California, schools. Jane stopped designing dresses for paper dolls and riding her bike to friends' houses. Her family decided that her depression and anger were so serious that the only alternative was to move.[8]*

*Cheltzie Hentz was seven and in second grade when she and other girls were tormented on the school bus. They were called names, taunted and threatened with a rubber knife. One of the girls said, "The boys called us sluts, bitches, and whores, and they teased me and my girlfriends because we didn't have penises; we only [had] vaginas."[9] The boys were all younger than ten.*

*Christine Franklin Kreeft was fifteen when a teacher had intercourse with her on school grounds. "The year before, he befriended me. I looked up to him and he was a teacher of mine. . . . And he would let me grade papers and tests and he would get me out of class to do these things. And for an entire year, that was how the relationship was. Then later on, it became obsessive when he would wait for me outside my classes, call me out of class."*

*He called her at home. "He asked me all kinds of questions about my boyfriend and he told me*

7

*[intimate things] about him and his wife. . . . It
was terrible. I mean I, I hated going to school. . . .
It was awful," Christine said.*[10]

◆ ◆ ◆

*"I felt so sick and ashamed. My counselor said I
should just get on with my life," Lisa Bye said. She
was in junior high and was being tormented by a
boy who grabbed at her shirt and crotch.*[11]

◆ ◆ ◆

Some victims choose to take legal action to stop the
sexual harassment. The families in most of these cases
did. Some families move to another town. Some
students change schools. Some students drop out of
school, never to return. Some end their lives.

Sexual harassment is not play. It is real and it is
serious. Its consequences can be paralyzing. It makes a
person feel powerless and unattractive. It hurts; it is
degrading. It can create anger, serious mental depression,
and low self-esteem.[12]

Sexual harassment can hinder learning and alter the
foundations of adulthood. It can cause grades to drop,
absenteeism to rise and plans for college to evaporate. Its
effects can last a lifetime.

Most people would not intentionally be hurtful.
Most teenagers appreciate humor and enjoy a good
laugh; they do not realize that what they consider to be
joking around may be taken by others as sexual harassment—but sometimes it is, and it can be devastating.

The injury is not always obvious. The injured person
does not wear a bandage or a cast. Sometimes even the

8

Comments and gestures directed at someone can turn something as simple as walking to class into a painful experience.

victims might not understand sexual harassment. They might not realize that the destructive feelings they are experiencing are being caused by the actions of others.

Some victims think that their own behavior brings on the sexual harassment. Adding insult to injury, victims are sometimes accused of being crazy, having an overactive imagination, or blowing things out of proportion.

There is also something else to consider: Sexual harassment is not only wrong, it is illegal.

So what exactly is sexual harassment? In some cases it is easy to identify, but in others it is not. However, even though the boundaries can be blurry, it is not impossible to understand.

With an open mind and an honest exploration of the subject, you can understand what sexual harassment is. You can stop participating in destructive acts and you can change questionable behavior. You can help friends understand its consequences and encourage them to find more appropriate ways to have fun. In the process, you can not only become more compassionate and understanding yourself, but you can also learn how victims cope with sexual harassment.

# 2

# What is Sexual Harassment?

Teenagers: Mothers think aliens took possession of their loving children; fathers think they should all be sent to military school; grandparents think the younger generation is going to hell in a handbasket. Teenagers are told this is the best time of their lives. Enjoy. So, being a teenager is cool. Right?

Not necessarily. Parents do not understand. Teachers are overburdened and out of touch. Teens are on the verge of adulthood, but many adults still see them and treat them as children. There is plenty of criticism and disapproval for teenagers, but not enough understanding and sympathy; their concerns often are brushed off as inconsequential "kid stuff."

Teens face worries far more serious than finding the right clothes or getting the newest CDs: They find that their own friends drive drunk and die, and that sex, one of the most exciting discoveries for teens, can kill.

As if that is not enough, in the grand conspiracy to make life complicated for teenagers another problem has surfaced—sexual harassment. Unfortunately, it is not always easy to identify because its definition can change depending upon the situation.

The fact that sexual harassment is difficult to identify does not change the severity of its consequences. If you have been sexually harassed or are guilty of sexually harassing someone, the consequences can be devastating.

Is it OK for a boy to whistle at a girl? Is it OK for a girl to flirt with a boy? Is there anything left that teenagers can do without getting into trouble? What is the difference between good, honest fun and sexual harassment?

Were the boys just having fun when they taunted seven-year-old Cheltzie Hentz, used nasty language, and threatened her with a rubber knife on the school bus? They thought so. Cheltzie did not.[1]

Were the boys just having fun when they sneaked up behind the eighth-grade girls, pulled down their skirts, and occasionally grabbed their breasts? They thought so. Judy Olson did not.[2]

Were the boys just having fun when they made "moo" sounds every day as thirteen-year-old Tawnya Brawdy, whose full-size bust had developed early, got off the school bus? They thought so. Tawnya did not.[3]

Were the members of the "Spur Posse" just having fun when they scored points for sexual encounters? They thought so. The girls who brought charges of rape and molestation against them did not.[4]

Were the boys who called sixth-grader Eve Bruneau obscene words just having fun when they ran their fingers down her back, found her bra, and snapped it? They thought so. Eve did not.[5]

Were the boys who tripped fifth-grader Jessica Hasenbank just having fun when they lay on top of her and put their hands on her private parts? They thought so. Jessica did not.[6]

Were the boys who called third-grader Jonathan Harms names and then pulled his pants down just having fun? They thought so. Jonathan did not.[7]

Were the girls and boys just having fun when they repeatedly asked eighth-grader Jane Doe what kind of a hot dog she preferred to have sex with? They thought so. Jane did not.[8]

## Is It Fun or Sexual Harassment?

What is the difference? That is easy: Sexual harassment is unwelcome and unwanted sexual behavior repeated often enough to create a hostile environment.[9] Defining sexual harassment becomes more difficult when we attempt to define "unwelcome." What one person calls unwelcome may be perfectly acceptable to another. Here are some clues:

- If the target appears to be upset, embarrassed, or uncomfortable, then the attention is unwelcome.

- If it would make you uncomfortable, or you would consider it unwelcome, the person receiving the attention probably feels the same way.

- If the target of the behavior did not "ask for" it or respond with similar behavior, it was probably unwelcome.[10] If you cannot tell by watching the person's reaction, find out.

## Intent and Impact

Assuming your behavior does not bother someone is not an excuse. The intent is not relevant. The impact determines whether it is sexual harassment.[11] Even though elementary-school-age children might not understand sexually offensive words and behavior in the same way that older students do, they do understand the effect of the words and actions on their targets.

In the Cheltzie Hentz case, the U.S. Department of Education Office of Civil Rights said:

> The fact that neither the boys nor the girls were sufficiently mature to realize all of the meanings and nuances of the language that was used does not obviate a finding that sexual harassment occurred. . . . In this case, there is no question that even the youngest girls understood that the language and conduct being used were expressions of hostility toward them on the basis of their gender.[12]

If an action is perceived as sexual harassment, it is sexual harassment. Some forms of sexual harassment are easy to identify: Forcing a kiss on someone is sexual harassment. Some forms are not so easy to identify. Is commenting on someone's clothing sexual harassment? Maybe. Maybe not. It is the responsibility of the person making the comment to find out.

We are all individuals. Just as our faces are uniquely ours, our perspectives, thoughts, and feelings are ours also. If you would not be offended or embarrassed by a certain action, that does not mean others would not be. And that would not mean, then, that the insult is the fault of the other person for being too sensitive or for overreacting.

Learning about effective relationships with others—from casual acquaintances to those we love—is a huge part of becoming an adult, and one of the most important things is to learn how not to hurt each other. Obviously, many adults never get it right. But caring and trying are giant steps in the right direction.

## Two Categories

There are basically two types of sexual harassment. One is easy to understand. It is called *quid pro quo,* which means something for something, one thing in return for another.

If a boy physically traps a girl and says, "Kiss me and I'll let you go," that is quid pro quo, something for something: You kiss me; I let you go. If a teacher asks for sexual favors in return for a good grade, that is quid pro quo, something for something: You give me sex; I give you a good grade.

The other type is more complicated. It is called hostile environment. One person, or a group of people, does not have the right to create an environment that is intimidating, hostile, or offensive to another person.[13] In other words, it is wrong—and illegal—to create a situation that offends someone so much that it is unpleasant, or even painful, for that person to walk down a hallway or ride a bus. That person has a right not to have his or her behavior limited in any way. Everyone has a right to an equal education. A hostile environment interferes with an individual's right to get an education.

Three elements constitute hostile environment sexual

One type of sexual harassment is hostile environment. This occurs when a person or group of people create an uncomfortable or intimidating environment for another person.

harassment. The actions must be sexual in nature, unwelcome or unwanted, and repeated.[14]

For sexual harassment to be considered quid pro quo all three elements need not be present—it is enough if there is only one incident, sexual in nature and unwanted. Even "welcome" sexual attention is sexual harassment in a student-teacher relationship because of a student's age and the legal requirement that the student be in school.

## Is It Flirting or Sexual Harassment?

What is the difference between sexual play, or flirting, and sexual harassment? Flirting is fun; it is an important part of teenage life. It is one of the ways boys and girls communicate with each other. Flirting feels good. Flirting changes to sexual harassment when power becomes part of the communication. When one person exercises power or control over another, flirting has changed to sexual harassment. Sexual harassment does not feel good.

Teenagers flirting are on equal footing—no power, no control, just equal give-and-take. He says, "Hey, you look pretty good today." She says, "Hey, you're not looking so bad yourself." There is equity. No one has the upper hand. No one is in control.

Sexual harassment is different. "Hey, you look pretty good today," he hollers down the hallway as a group of boys laugh. She says nothing because they are not on equal footing. If she says, "Drop dead," she knows it will encourage not only more jokes and comments from him, but from the whole group. So, she says nothing.

If this scenario is repeated often enough to alter the

# Sexual Harassment

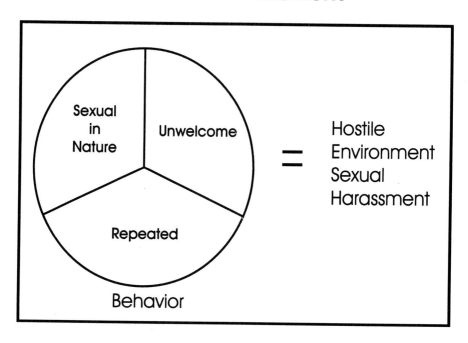

Behavior must be sexual in nature, unwelcome, and repeated to constitute hostile environment sexual harassment.

girl's environment, the boy has the upper hand. He has control over her behavior because of feared consequences. Sexual harassment is power and control. Flirting is not.

## What about Bullying?

Sometimes boys and girls tease one another to communicate. Teasing is like flirting—there is equality. No one has the upper hand; no one is in control. Teasing becomes bullying when power and control are involved. Boys bully boys. Boys bully girls. Girls bully boys. Girls bully girls. It happens in all combinations and it is wrong.

Is bullying sexual harassment? It is unwanted and it is often repeated, but is it sexual in nature? Bullying is not sexual harassment unless it is unwanted, repeated and involves a person's gender.

## Sexist Comments and Language

Sexism is prejudice against members of one sex by the other and is often evident in what we say. Sexist comments create limitations because of gender: Women cannot be generals and men cannot nurture children. One sexist comment is not sexual harassment, but a pattern of unwelcome sexist comments or jokes is.

Sexist language supports attitudes that stereotype people by gender or assume that the male is more important than the female: manpower, man the office, men at work, repairman, servicemen.[15] If sexist language is used frequently and it creates a hostile or demeaning environment, it is sexual harassment.

19

## Is Swearing Sexual Harassment?

The use of nonsexual swear words is not sexual harassment. If repeated often enough, a hostile environment could be created. That would be considered harassment, but not sexual harassment. The use of sexual swear words, however, if unwelcome and repeated, does constitute sexual harassment.

## What is Sexual Discrimination?

Discrimination is showing partiality or prejudice in the way a person or a group of people is treated. Sexual discrimination is treating someone differently because of his or her gender, as in the following examples: A teacher chooses only boys for a math team because boys usually perform better in math than girls; a student is singled out for special treatment on the basis of gender biases (boys are better at science so Joey will run the experiment, not Mary) rather than the student's individual performance;[16] or, funding for girls' high school and college athletic programs is not equal to funding for boys' programs simply because sports are considered more important in the education of boys than of girls.

The courts have ruled that sexual harassment is a form of sexual discrimination. In the case *Meritor Savings Bank* v. *Vinson*, the U.S. Supreme Court acknowledged that sexual harassment is prohibited under Title VII of the Civil Rights Act of 1964. The Court said that if a supervisor sexually harassed a subordinate because of his or her sex, the supervisor discriminated on the basis of sex.[17]

Sexual harassment is similar to racism. Racism is what we most often think of when we hear the word discrimination. Minorities should not be forced to endure racial slurs just as all people should not be forced to hear sexual remarks.

## Learn to Spot It

The best way to recognize sexual harassment is to apply the definition: Is the behavior sexual in nature, is it unwelcome, and in the case of hostile environment, is it repeated?

According to a study commissioned by the American Association of University Women Educational Foundation, the following forms of sexual harassment are experienced most frequently in schools:

- Making sexual comments, jokes, gestures, or looks.
- Touching, grabbing, or pinching in a sexual way.
- Intentionally brushing against a person in a sexual way.
- Flashing (exposing one's genitals).
- Mooning (exposing one's buttocks).
- Spreading sexual rumors.
- Pulling clothing in a sexual way.
- Pulling clothing off or down.
- Showing, giving, or displaying sexual photographs, illustrations, cartoons, messages, notes, or pornography.
- Writing sexual messages/graffiti about a person on bathroom walls, in locker rooms, etc.
- Forcing a kiss on someone.
- Forcing someone to do something sexual.
- Calling someone gay or lesbian.
- Spying on someone who is dressing or showering.[18]

21

With the exceptions of forcing a kiss on someone and forcing someone to do something sexual, these behaviors need to be repeated in order to be called sexual harassment.

More examples of sexually harassing behaviors have been reported in American high schools:

- Commenting about parts of the body, what type of sex the victim would be "good at," clothing, looks, etc.
- Using the computer to leave sexual messages or graffiti or to play sexually offensive computer games.
- Pressuring for sexual activity.
- Cornering, blocking, standing too close, or following.
- Showing R-rated movies during class.
- Giving snuggies or wedgies (pulling underwear up at the waist so it goes in between the buttocks).
- Spiking (pulling down someone's pants).
- Unwelcome massaging of the neck or shoulders.
- Touching oneself sexually in front of others.
- Making kissing sounds or smacking sounds, licking the lips suggestively, howling, catcalling, or whistling.
- Repeatedly asking someone out when he or she is not interested.
- Circulating slam books (lists of students' names with derogatory sexual comments written about them by other students).
- Sexual assault or attempted sexual assault.
- Rape.[19]

These lists are not inclusive. Just because something is not on one of these lists, it does not mean the behavior

Giving someone a wedgie might get you a laugh, but it might also get you into serious trouble. The behavior, if repeated, is sexual harassment.

is not sexual harassment. They are only to be used as guidelines. The lists make it clear that there are different types as well as varying degrees of sexual harassment, including teacher-to-student, student-to-student, and harassment by a group, but there are also other types, such as favoritism and student-to-teacher sexual harassment.

Favoritism is when a student receives preferential treatment because of his or her submission to a teacher's requests for sexual advances. The object of the attention is a victim of sexual harassment. The other students in the class are being discriminated against because they are not receiving the same preferential treatment.[20] There can also be favoritism from a teacher who is attracted to a student but does not actually act on it. In this case, the other students in the class are the victims of discrimination.

Student-to-teacher harassment is when a student harasses a teacher. Examples would be: students making sexually explicit comments to a staff member; students placing sexually explicit materials in a classroom where the teacher will find them; students making obscene phone calls to a teacher.[21]

Test yourself. Are the following situations examples of sexual harassment?

A. A teacher repeatedly makes suggestive comments to a student.

B. A teacher propositions a student one time.

C. A student is depicted in sexually explicit cartoons circulated in a classroom.

D. Someone a student does not like asks him or her for a date.

# Teens Sexually Harassed at School

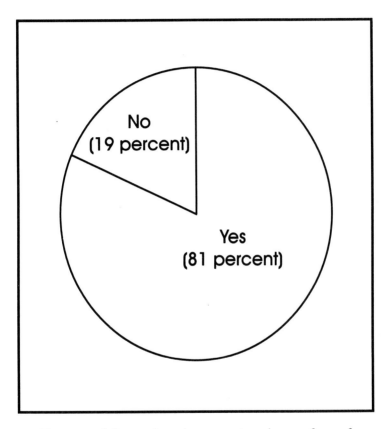

No
(19 percent)

Yes
(81 percent)

Four out of five students have experienced some form of sexual harassment at school, according to the American Association of University Women survey *Hostile Hallways*.

**Answers:**

A. Yes. Repeated suggestive comments from either peers or a teacher can create a hostile learning environment.

B. Yes. Because of a student's age, and the definition of quid pro quo sexual harassment, any sexual proposition by a teacher to a student is sexual harassment.

C. Yes. Circulating cartoons of a sexual nature about someone can create a hostile learning environment.

D. No. Someone asking another person out is not sexual harassment. However, if that person bothers another by continuously asking for a date after the person has made it clear that he or she is not interested, that is sexual harassment.

When recognizing sexual harassment, keep in mind that feelings and thoughts are warning signals. You could be a victim of sexual harassment if you are thinking:

"I can't believe this is happening to me."

"Why me? What did I do?"

"I wish I could make it stop."

"If I say anything, everyone will think I'm crazy."

"Just leave me alone."

"What's going to happen next?"

"I wish I could get away."

"Why doesn't anyone help me?"

"I hate you for doing this."[22]

You could be a victim of sexual harassment if you are feeling: alone, scared, hopeless, frightened, angry, helpless, guilty, or confused.[23] Trust your thoughts and feelings. Do something about them.

# 3

# How Did We Get Here?

*When Sybilla Masters applied for a patent for her invention, it was issued to her husband because the law did not allow women to receive patents. "On Nov. 25, 1715, the government gave a patent to Masters's husband, for 'the sole use and benefit of a new invention . . . by Sybilla, his wife, for cleaning and curing the Indian Corn growing in the several colonies in America.'" Women in the colonies were not allowed to receive patents or to vote. Married women were not allowed to own land.[1]*

*When Susan B. Anthony (1820–1906) voted in the 1872 presidential election, she was arrested, tried, convicted, and fined. Women did not have the right to vote in 1872.[2]*

*Sojourner Truth (1797–1883) was born into slavery. In her famous "Ain't I A Woman?" speech delivered in 1851 at the Women's Convention in Akron, Ohio, she addressed the injustices she had suffered as a black woman. She lived at a time when the word "slave" meant "man" and the word "woman" meant "white middle class." Black women were referred to by more degrading terms, if referred to at all.*

*"Look at my arm! I have ploughed and planted and gathered into barns . . . and ain't I a woman? I could work as much and eat as much as a man—when I could get it—and bear the lash as well. . . . I have borne thirteen children and seen most of ' em sold into slavery, and when I cried out with my mother's grief, none but Jesus helped me—and ain't I a woman?"*[3]

*Lucretia Mott (1793–1880) was denied a seat at the 1840 Anti-Slavery Convention in London because she was a woman. Because of the incident, she helped organize the famous Seneca Falls convention of 1848 in which, for the first time, American women demanded equal rights under the law.*[4]

*Prudence Crandall (1803–1890), a Connecticut schoolmistress, was arrested and imprisoned for admitting a young black woman to her school and announcing her plans to set up a school for black girls.*[5]

*Deborah Sampson Gannett (1760–1827) disguised herself as a man and used the name Robert Shirtliff to serve her country in the Continental Army. She participated in several battles as a member of the Massachusetts regiment, hiding when she was wounded. When she was hospitalized with typhoid fever her sex was discovered and she was discharged from the army.*[6]

*Author, reformer, and feminist Frances Wright (1795–1852) supported her husband throughout their fifteen-year marriage; when she divorced him, he was given all her property.*[7]

*Elizabeth Blackwell (1821–1910), the first woman in the United States to receive a medical degree, was turned down by many medical schools because she was a woman. The administration at the Geneva Medical School of New York left her admission up to the students. The students, thinking it a hoax, voted to admit her. When she graduated at the top of her class, they changed their minds.*[8]

*Sarah M. Grimke (1792–1873) and her sister, Angelina, were the first women to speak out against slavery and then for women's rights. As Quakers in Charleston, South Carolina, they were publicly scorned for their outspokenness. Appalled by the sexism they found in the abolitionist movement, they devoted equal time to women's rights.*[9]

*Abigail Adams (1744–1818), long before Hillary Rodham Clinton, is said to have been a near equal partner in her marriage to John Adams. She influenced the decisions made by both John Adams, her husband, and John Quincy Adams, their son, during their respective presidencies. In one of her letters to her husband, whom she addressed as "Dear Friend," she said: "Remember the Ladies, and be more generous and favorable to them than your ancestors. Do not put such unlimited power into the hands of the Husbands. . . . If particular care and attention is not paid to the Laidies [sic] we are determined to foment a Rebellion."[10]*

*Amelia Bloomer (1818–1894) addressed a very basic problem for women—underwear so constricting that it was dangerous, whalebone stays that poked into the body, and yards of hot, heavy fabric that made movement difficult. Bloomer suggested, as a less restrictive alternative, the "Turkish trouser," full-cut pantaloons worn under a short skirt (hence the name "bloomers"). She helped set a course for the free-fitting clothing that women enjoy today. She also published the* Lily, *a women's newspaper that was probably the first to be edited entirely by a woman.*[11]

*Margaret Sanger (1883–1966) addressed a much more serious issue. In 1912, dispensing information about ways to avoid pregnancy was illegal and*

*female contraception was barely existent. Typically, the neighborhood abortionist, charging five dollars, would consult and treat more than a hundred women on a Saturday night. Working as a visiting nurse on the Lower East Side of New York City, Sanger was outraged by the conditions in which she found women after these surgeries, many of whom died. She felt the pain and hopelessness of women whose bodies had been depleted by successive pregnancies—some as many as twenty or more. She left nursing and sought practical methods of "birth control," a phrase she coined, that could be available to all women. She believed that birth control was a fundamental human right—a right for which she continually fought with government and organized religion.*[12]

All of these women experienced sexual discrimination, even though it did not have a name.

## The Way It Is Now

The Nineteenth Amendment to the U.S. Constitution was ratified in time for women to vote in the 1920 presidential election. It says: "The right of citizens of the United States to vote shall not be denied or abridged by the United States or by any state on account of sex."[13]

In 1963, Betty Friedan wrote *The Feminine Mystique.* The book clearly defined American women's greatest problems and was seen by many as a catalyst to a new wave of the women's movement. Friedan was founder and first president of the National Organization for Women (NOW).

On August 26, 1970, the fiftieth anniversary of the Nineteenth Amendment, Gloria Steinem, feminist and author, joined Friedan in the Women's Strike for Equality. For the first time in this country, the reality of women's political power was exhibited.[14]

In 1963, two women had seats in the U.S. Senate and nineteen women sat in the House.[15] Over thirty years later, in 1996, there were eight women senators and forty-seven women representatives.[16]

With the blossoming of political power and the wide accessibility of birth control methods, women's roles have changed drastically.

The Civil Rights Act of 1964, Title VII, prohibited sexual and racial discrimination at work.

The Civil Rights Act of 1972, Title IX of the Federal Education Amendments, prohibited sexual and racial discrimination against students and staff.[17]

In 1972, an Equal Rights Amendment was proposed. It said, "Equality of rights under the law shall not be denied or abridged by the United States or by any state on account of sex." The amendment would have reinforced rights granted to all citizens by the due process and equal protection clauses of the Fifth and Fourteenth Amendments. It also would have placed equal responsibility on all citizens and all legislation would have had to apply equally to both sexes. The amendment was defeated in 1982 after a ten-year struggle for ratification.[18]

What we now call sexual harassment was formerly considered a personal problem of individuals; as a result, the victim was often blamed. Many considered this behavior unavoidable in mostly-male workplaces.

As more and more women began sharing their experiences, they realized that this was not a problem to be dealt with individually: This widespread and systemic abuse required national attention.[19]

In 1980, the Equal Employment Opportunity Commission issued guidelines that defined sexual harassment as a form of sexual discrimination. That same year, in *Continental Can* v. *Minnesota,* the Minnesota Supreme Court ruled that an organization or employer was liable for sexual harassment and must take prompt action to correct the problem.[20]

In 1986, the U.S. Supreme Court stated in *Meritor Savings Bank* v. *Vinson* that sexual harassment was a form of sexual discrimination.[21]

In 1992, the U.S. Supreme Court determined that if a student was sexually harassed, he or she could seek monetary damages and demand other remedies from schools and school officials (*Franklin* v. *Gwinnett County Public Schools*).[22]

## The Way It Should Be

Although sexual harassment was not always named as such, it nevertheless existed and limited women's opportunities. Fortunately, now that the issues have been brought forward, defined and discussed, women are moving closer to becoming equal members of society. The goal is a society that does not discriminate against any of its members, one that is enriched because each member has the opportunity to contribute to the maximum of his or her abilities.

We are getting closer.

33

# 4

# Who is Guilty?

She was fifteen, a sophomore in high school, and a stall in the boys' bathroom was named after her. It was the "Katy stall." The messages left nothing to the imagination: "Katie Lyle [blanks] dogs," "Katie Lyle is a whore," "Katie Lyle is a sex slave." The message of the graffiti writers, who had misspelled her name, found its way to the hallways and classrooms. "People would yell things at me across the hall [such as] 'I went to the bathroom in your stall this morning, Katy.'"

Her girlfriends told her she was overreacting, that she should make light of it. They said it should not bother her.

But it did. She went home every day and cried. She hated school. This went on for eighteen months.

After repeated requests to the principal failed to stop

Graffiti is sexual harassment if the content or illustrations are sexual in nature.

the harassment, Katy filed a lawsuit against the school. The school was accused of tolerating the peer-to-peer sexual harassment that Katy suffered at school. The case was settled out of court and Katy was paid fifteen thousand dollars by the Duluth (Minnesota) Public Schools.[1]

## Is There Ink on Your Hands?

Are you guilty of sexual harassment without knowing it? Could you have added a catchy line in the "Katy stall" thinking that since there were so many already, what difference could it make? Would you think circulating an obscene picture with a classmate's name under it was harmless? Would you think a limerick written about one of your classmates was funny, pass it on, and laugh with the next person who read it?

Most harassment in schools is committed by students. According to the American Association of University Women's report *Hostile Hallways*, nearly four out of five (79 percent) students reporting that they have been sexually harassed were harassed by a current or former student.[2]

Girls report being harassed by (from most often to least often): a male acting alone, a group of males, a mixed group of males and females, a female acting alone, a group of females.

Boys report being harassed by (from most often to least often): a female acting alone, a group of females, a male acting alone, a group of males, a mixed group of females and males.

Another interesting bit of information from the survey is the number of students who admitted that they

36

Circulating notes or illustrations about someone that are sexual in nature is sexual harassment.

had sexually harassed someone. Two thirds (66 percent) of all boys and more than half (52 percent) of all girls surveyed said they had sexually harassed someone at school.[3]

They gave the following reasons:

- It is just part of school life; a lot of people do it; it is no big deal.

- I thought the person liked it.

- I wanted a date with the person.

- My friends encouraged me, pushed me into doing it.

- I wanted something from that person.

- I wanted the person to think I had some sort of power over him or her.[4]

## How Can You Know Whether You Are Guilty?

First, care. If you are asking this question, you most likely do care and want to avoid causing anyone pain, embarrassment, or emotional injury. After all, what can you gain by hurting someone? Nothing, but you have something to lose.

Second, observe. Look with an honest eye and an open mind at your own actions and motivations and at the other person's reaction. What is behind your actions? Learn about yourself by trying to determine your motives and learn about others by trying to understand their feelings.

Third, put yourself in the other person's place. If the roles were reversed, would it cause you any anger, embarrassment or shame? Of course, this is not foolproof since

# Who Are Teens
# Sexually Harassed By?

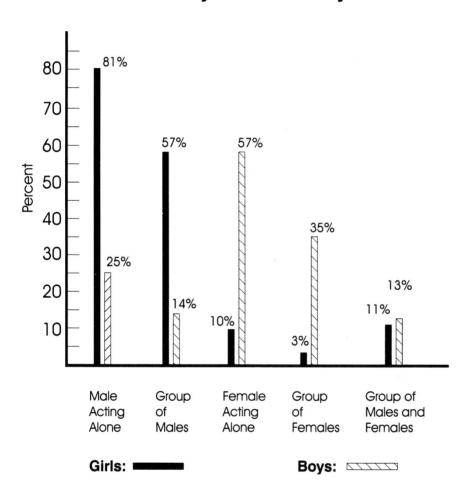

Girls: ▬▬▬▬  Boys: ▨▨▨▨

Most sexual harassment in schools is committed by students. According to *Hostile Hallways*, some students reported being sexually harassed in more than one situation.

we are individuals and one person's reaction might not be the same as another person's.

Fourth, get another opinion. Talk to an independent observer, a friend, or an older brother or sister.

Fifth, ask. If you are still not sure whether your actions are hurtful, ask the person receiving your attention.

## Are You Really Funny?

Humor is great. Everyone loves to be around people who have a good sense of humor. We all like to laugh with our friends and humor is a great way to break the ice with people we do not know.

Unfortunately, humor is sometimes directed at someone, and that is often what makes it funny. We have all heard ethnic and racist jokes, sexist jokes, and dirty jokes.

If you tell a dirty joke, are you guilty of sexual harassment? One dirty joke is not sexual harassment. Two dirty jokes are not sexual harassment. Repeated joking at someone's expense can be. If your humor is based on a person's sex, is unwelcome, and is repeated often enough to create a hostile environment, it is sexual harassment.

If you either suspect or have been told that your sexual humor is unwelcome or unappreciated, it could be sexual harassment.

As we have already learned, the intent of the harasser is irrelevant. It is the impact of the action that is important. Several people can interpret the same situation differently. Each person's sensitivities must be respected.

If your humor is not unwelcome, it is not sexual harassment, even if it is sexual in nature.

## Do You Succumb to Mob Mentality?

If you have ever been talked into doing something by several friends, you understand the power and dynamic of the group. Usually it is harmless. You were persuaded to go to a movie when you really wanted to cruise the mall, or your friends decided to go to the arcade when you really preferred to go to the park. You went along anyway because you wanted to hang out with your friends more than anything else—in the long run, it did not really matter.

Sometimes the decision made by the group is a bad one and once group action gets a little momentum, it takes on a life of its own.

Four members of the Chronics, a group of Seneca Valley High School students in Germantown, Maryland, were accused of rape. One was accused of raping a fourteen-year-old girl who allegedly had been pushed into a laundry room while his friends prevented her girlfriends from helping her.

Three Chronics allegedly pulled another fourteen-year-old girl into a basement utility room at a party and took turns raping her. The girl reported that the boy who raped her first told her, "Whatever you do to me, you have to do to my boys."[5]

Sometimes we do things in groups that we would never think about doing on our own, sometimes because there is safety in numbers, sometimes because a group provides anonymity and a feeling of acceptance.

Sexual harassment by groups of either boys or girls is common on school campuses. Some of the types most often reported are: mooning; spiking; flipping (males

Intentionally flipping someone's skirt up is not innocent fun; it is sexual harassment.

lifting a girl's skirt up); flashing or sharking (a male breaking away from a group of his friends and biting a female on the breast); cornering, blocking, standing too close, or following; giving snuggies or wedgies; touching oneself sexually in front of others; howling, catcalling, or whistling.[6]

Each member of a group is guilty of the behavior of the group. Although you may feel an anonymity, detachment, or even powerlessness because you do not condone what the group is doing, you are guilty if you remain part of the group.

43

# 5

# What Can You Do About It?

The water begins to churn, a vortex develops, the human-powered wave machine is at work. Teenage boys with locked arms move in circles, churning the water and creating a whirlpool.

Whirlpools have been a part of summer fun in inner New York City swimming pools for years. Being splashed or dunked was the worst thing that could happen, but a new twist has developed. Girls surrounded in the whirling, bubbling water have been fondled and have had their bathing suits pulled off.

One hot summer day in 1993 at the South Bronx pool, a fourteen-year-old girl was surrounded, her bathing suit top was removed, and a finger was inserted into her vagina.[1]

If you were one of the boys locked arm-in-arm with

the others but never touched anyone, are you guilty? If you knew that your friend was touching someone inappropriately, are you guilty? If you knew the goal of the game was to trap girls and that something could happen to them, are you guilty? If you were part of the group only because you did not want the others to think you were a bad sport, are you guilty?

Obviously, if you were the one doing the touching, you are guilty. What you may not realize is that you are also guilty if you helped create a situation that enabled sexual harassment to take place. So what do you do? What exactly is your responsibility when the group's behavior crosses the line?

If you are in a position of leadership in the group, you can point out that it is not cool and suggest that it be stopped. But what if you are not one of the leaders of the group? Sometimes offering an alternative works. Challenge someone to a race. Offer to get the volleyball. Suggest anything that changes the direction of the group's energy.

If that does not work, or if it is not a realistic alternative, leave; maybe a few others will follow. Then, at least, you are not guilty of participating in the offense. If it is a situation in which help should be summoned or authorities notified, do so. It can be done anonymously. Your action might stop the escalation of sexual harassment into sexual assault (unwanted touching), which is a crime.

If you are a bystander, you may feel helpless. But there are a few things you can do, especially in situations where the harasser is an individual rather than a group. You can say that you do not think it is funny, tell the person to stop, or walk away.

Girls have been sexually harassed in swimming pools. Boys, locked
arm-in-arm, create whirlpools, harass, and sometimes molest the
girls trapped in the churning water.

Do not say or do anything that encourages the harasser. Do not laugh, stare at the person being harassed, joke, or gossip about what happened. These actions could aggravate the situation and make people think you approve and are participating in the harassment.[2]

You have a responsibility neither to encourage nor to engage in group behavior that has become sexual harassment. Each individual is accountable for his or her behavior. It is your responsibility to choose not to participate.

## Do You Protect Your Image?

It takes courage to refuse to participate in things your friends are engaged in. No one wants to be considered a bad sport, a prude, or "too good" for the others. No one wants his or her sense of humor or sense of adventure questioned.

Refusing to participate does set you apart and makes a statement about how you feel about what is happening. It is judgmental. But in some situations, it is the only right thing to do.

The group is not always engaged in behavior that is inappropriate. Be an active part of the group when the activity is not harmful. But if it shifts in the wrong direction, do the right thing. There are appropriate ways to demonstrate one's loyalty or identity with a group. Being party to sexual harassment is not one of them. Choose another way. The group that continually engages in sexual harassment is not the group for you.

We are identified by the friends we keep. Choose friends who can have fun without putting others down, friends who can have fun without hurting others, and friends who do not enjoy sexually harassing other students.

## Do You Laugh When You Should Not?

When something is funny it is hard not to laugh, especially when the joke is delivered by a natural storyteller. Some people have a talent for telling jokes and sometimes whether or not their material is appropriate, you laugh. So how do you tell someone that their material is not appropriate? One approach would be to change the direction of the conversation—change the topic.

If the harasser does not get the message, tell him or her you do not think it is funny, that it is out-of-line or that it is not the right time or place. Point out that something appropriate in one group of people may not be appropriate in another.

Another tactic is to not laugh. If the harasser's audience does not laugh, the joke is immediately a flop. There is not much satisfaction in telling jokes if no one laughs. An alternative is to leave. Do not participate in humor that sexually harasses someone.

## Do You Pretend It Is OK?

Sometimes, it is such a relief not to be the one who is targeted that your sense of responsibility is at complete rest. Remember that the identity of the target often is not important—it could just as easily be you.

According to the National School Safety Counsel, the identity of the victim is not important because the goal of the activity is to prove masculinity. Strong peer support is reported in most accounts of sexual harassment. The offenders are often cheered and egged on.[3]

If you are not in a position to influence the harasser to stop, do not try, but by all means do not laugh. Do not stare at the person being harassed; do not encourage the harasser or do anything that could be interpreted as your approval or participation. If harassment persists, walk away. Do not pretend it is OK because it is not directed at you. It is not.[4]

## Support the Victim

If you are a friend of someone who has been sexually harassed, be a good listener. A friend can sometimes be more help than anyone else. A friend can help sort out what has happened and give advice.

Remember, though, never act on your own without permission. That would only make your friend feel more powerless; instead, help your friend decide what to do and be supportive. For example, your friend may wish to discuss the problem with an adult. You can help your friend prepare what to say and help get the details straight. Write down: "what happened; when and where it occurred; who saw it; how it made your friend feel; how your friend tried to stop it. Provide plenty of detail. Offer to go along" when the incident is reported. "Your friend may be scared and really need your support. Be reassuring. But let your friend do the talking."[5]

How a victim feels about himself or herself depends on how he or she is treated by others: Is the victim believed or dismissed, supported or discredited? Our society tends to blame the victim. Blaming the victim removes the responsibility from the harasser and decreases our own sense of vulnerability. One thinks, in effect, "It is Mary's fault that she is treated that way. Look at the way she dresses. I am not like Mary."[6]

When Sam Harms first met with the principal to discuss the sexual harassment his son, Jonathan, was

# Who Do Teens Tell About Sexual Harassment?

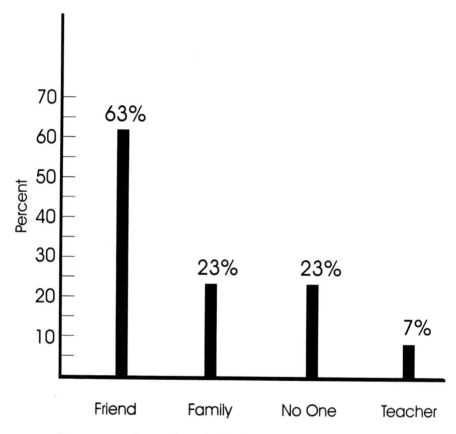

Teens most frequently tell friends about sexual harassment. According to *Hostile Hallways*, the total number of reported cases is over 100 percent because sometimes students reported sexual harassment to more than one person.

experiencing at school, the principal said, "Why don't you have your son psychologically tested so that maybe we'll have an understanding of why the boys treat him like they do."[7]

Blaming the victim permits society to label sexual harassment as the victim's problem rather than as society's problem.

To support victims of sexual harassment, Barbara Chester, a specialist on the subject of victimization, recommends the following:

- Define the experience as sexual harassment. Do not call it teasing if it is sexual harassment. Call it what it is.

- Assure confidentiality. Make sure the victim understands that whatever she or he chooses to tell you will stay between the two of you.

- Recognize the sense of grief and loss. Realize the victim has been violated. Try to relate to that.

- Provide a safe environment. If the victim needs some space before going home, provide the place and time. Go to your own house for a while. Go get a soda. Do whatever makes the victim feel safe.

- Reassure the victim. Try to identify with the experience and reassure the victim that his or her thoughts and feelings are right; what happened was wrong.

- Provide choices so the victim regains some sense of empowerment. Ask how she or he wants to proceed. Offer alternatives.

- Do not press for immediate decisions. Make sure the victim knows that you are available when he or she is ready to take action.

- Listen respectfully. Do not interrupt. Just listen. Allow for pauses in conversation. Sometimes when we speak only to fill pauses, we are not allowing the person who should be talking a chance to get a word in. Silences in conversation are OK.

• Be nonjudgmental. Do not try to put a value judgment on what happened to the person or what the person is feeling.

• Validate feelings and sense of self-worth. Try to help the victim understand that the thoughts and feelings he or she is experiencing are valid, based on what happened to him or her.

• Help the victim understand that what happened was not his or her fault. He or she did nothing to deserve what happened. The person was at the wrong place at the wrong time.

• Respect personal timing regarding ability to cope. If the victim makes the choice to wait or not to do anything, respect the choice, even if you do not agree. If the person needs more time, respect that need.

• Familiarize yourself with outside agencies. Be ready to help the victim move forward with reporting the incident and getting help to cope with the incident. Find out who can help at your school and in your community. Never push the victim to get help, but be ready with the information just in case he or she asks for it.[8]

# 6

# What Characteristics Create the Victim?

They were teenagers, good athletes, and friends who enjoyed high school football games, parties, and playing basketball after school.

They wore San Antonio Spurs caps and were tagged the Spur Posse. The big men on campus, they thought everybody looked up to them.

It gave them a particular thrill to keep track of their sexual encounters, a boy scoring a point for each girl he had sex with. Although the boys denied any negative impact of their behavior, claiming it to be merely part of dating and good times, some of the girls alleged that Spur Posse members used persuasion and threats to obtain sexual favors. The Los Angeles County Sheriff's investigators said the Lakewood High School gang in

Lakewood, California, victimized a number of young women.

The Spur Posse members denied that anyone was pressured into having sex, but admitted that names of willing girls were shared.[1]

Eight of the boys were arrested for investigation of rape and molestation of at least seven girls. They were released when the investigation concluded that the sex had been consensual.[2]

Days later, however, a ninth boy pleaded guilty to one count of molestation.[3] One month later, a second teen was charged with child molestation. A third youth served one hundred hours of community service to clear himself of child molestation charges.[4]

## Who Are the Victims?

Anyone can be a victim of sexual harassment: girls and boys, children, teens, and adults. A majority of eighth to eleventh grade students in American public schools have experienced sexual harassment.

According to one report, 85 percent of girls and 76 percent of boys surveyed said they had experienced some form of sexual harassment during their school lives.

The gender gap widens when the frequency of the harassment is considered. Nearly one in three (31 percent) girls has experienced unwanted advances "often," compared with less than one in five (18 percent) boys. According to the same report:

> A student's first experience of sexual harassment is most likely to occur in the middle school/junior high years of 6th through 9th grade: 47% of the students who have been harassed fall into this

54

group—40% of boys and 54% of girls. One-third of those students (32%) who have been harassed first experienced such unwelcome behavior before 7th grade. For girls, the percentage is 34; for boys, 32.[5]

## Special-needs Students

Special-education teens are at a greater risk of being sexually harassed by other students because of their increased vulnerability. They feel a loss of power and self-esteem and are unclear about where their boundaries end and others' begin.[6]

They are easy targets. Because they do not always understand their own boundaries, they also do not know they should report any inappropriate treatment. They may know it does not feel right, but they do not always have the ability to identify what has happened to them as sexual harassment. They do not understand that they have a right to demand it be stopped.

## Is She Too Masculine, He Too Feminine?

Queer, fag, faggot, fruit, homo, fairy, wimp, sissy. Long before boys and girls understand their own sexuality, much less their sexual orientation, they toss these words around. They are negative tags, degrading and hurtful.

Some boys think that one of the worst insults a boy can receive is to be accused of being like a girl. This is because both boys and girls clearly receive the message that girls are not worthy of respect. The message is also loud and clear that exerting power over girls, and other weaker boys, is appropriate behavior for boys.[7]

Boys who do not conform to male stereotypes are more likely to be victims of sexual harassment. A boy may be seen to show too much sensitivity. In our culture, sensitivity is considered a girl thing, so boys may emphasize masculinity to be as different from girls as possible. Boys are pressured to adopt the behavior of their peers to avoid being sexually harassed by their peers.[8]

Girls who are too independent or sure of themselves are seen as masculine. In our culture, independence and self-assurance is considered a boy thing. These qualities may make girls targets for sexual harassment by other girls as well as boys. Girls who are physically stronger or more athletic can also become targets of sexual harassment. If you do not fit the female stereotype, which is very narrowly defined, then you are a likely target. According to the *Hostile Hallways* report:

> Students say they would be very upset if they were called gay or lesbian. Being called gay would be more upsetting to boys than actual physical abuse. . . . 17% of students say they have been called lesbian or gay when they didn't want to be—10% of girls and 23% of boys . . . Of those boys who have been called gay, more than half (58%) say they have called someone else gay.[9]

Homosexual teenagers are in a high-risk group. In many schools, "fag" and "queer" are everyday insults; many older teens readily abuse—verbally or physically—anyone suspected of being gay. Even some teachers and school executives show hostility.[10] Sexual harassment against homosexuals is not clearly defined by law.

In May 1993, the Massachusetts Board of Education endorsed a plan that suggested that schools statewide

Females can be victims of sexual harassment if they are viewed by their peers as either too feminine or too masculine.

"adopt policies that promote sensitivity to homosexual students and provide in-school-counseling services for the youths and their families." The board made this decision:

> [B]ased in part on a report by Governor William Weld's Commission on Gay and Lesbian Youth that showed that homosexuals nationwide were being persecuted in school—leading to isolation and depression and making them account for 28 percent of high school dropouts and one-third of teenage suicides.[11]

Somerville High School in Somerville, Massachusetts, allowed the formation of a support group for gay students. "What we heard over and over again is that these young people feel frightened to be in school. Many youths became so fearful that classmates would abuse them that they chose not to go. We hope to counter the isolation and prevent suicides by providing support and guidance through teachers," David LaFontaine, chairman of the Board of Education in Somerville, has said.[12]

Danny Martinez, a gay student at Somerville High, said the group helped build his confidence. "I feel relieved because you can get together and say anything. It's a relief not to have it bottled up inside of you, to not have to be quiet for the rest of your life."[13]

Troix Battencourt, eighteen, said he dropped out of Lowell (Massachusetts) High School even though he was class president and a varsity soccer player. He could not handle living a lie. When he came out (openly stated his homosexuality), his mother kicked him out of the house. "I wouldn't have dropped out" if there had been a support group, he said. "I wouldn't have felt so isolated."[14]

While serving as U.S. Surgeon General, Joycelyn Elders called homophobia "a public health issue." She said teenage gay and lesbian suicides, drug and alcohol use, and depression are linked to some Americans' refusal to accept homosexuality.

"It's important not to blame the victim," Elders said. "They [homosexual teens] are also more often the targets of school violence and physical violence at home."[15]

Thirty percent of all teens who commit suicide are gay, and gay teens are two to three times more likely than other teens to attempt suicide, according to a 1989 report by the U.S. Department of Health and Human Services.[16] An article in *Education Digest* says:

> The American Academy of Pediatrics has urged members to provide services to gay youth; the National Education Association says every school should provide counseling to gay students; and the Child Welfare League of America, a major children's advocacy group, urges efforts to help gay youth.[17]

Schools have a responsibility to assure gay teens the same safe environment they would assure any other minority, protecting them from the abuse common against homosexuals.[18]

## Are Good Students Nerds, Geeks, Dorks, or Dweebs?

Boys who are good students are often perceived as weaker. Sometimes they are physically weaker; sometimes they are just different from the pack because they have other priorities.

American culture does not place the same importance

on academic excellence that it does on physical excellence. If a boy does not perform in some sport or physical activity, he is seen as weaker than those who do. If a boy is lucky enough to excel both academically and in sports, he is safe. But often, excelling academically puts a boy in the weaker category and sets him up for sexual harassment by his peers.

Girls have mixed feelings about being good students. If being a good student makes one less popular, many girls are not interested. Girls who are good students are sometimes perceived as being too independent or too sure of themselves. This translates into being "more masculine," which boys often find threatening or competitive, but not attractive.

Sixth- and seventh-grade girls surveyed for the American Association of University Women report *How Schools Shortchange Girls*, rate being well-liked and popular as more important than being perceived as independent or competent.[19]

"Girls who drop out of school are more likely to hold traditional gender-role stereotypes than are girls who graduate. Female dropouts are more likely to believe a woman's role is in the home, not in the work force," the report says.[20]

"Boys and girls view academic failure very differently. Boys often attribute their failures to lack of trying and feel that more effort is needed to be successful. Girls are more likely to attribute their failures to a simple lack of ability."[21]

Girls who are good students become especially threatening when they move into territory traditionally dominated by boys. "Females and males abandon math and science for different reasons. Males who drop out of math and science tend to do so because of a lack of competence—they cannot do the work; many females who drop out do so even though they can do the work," the report says.[22] The stigma that comes along with excelling in math and science classes is not worth it to many girls.

Also, girls suffer increased sexual harassment when they enroll in nontraditional courses. Excelling in those courses only makes it worse.

Nan D. Stein, educator and civil rights specialist, tells the story of sixteen-year-old Joanne, the only girl in an auto mechanics class at a vocational school. She was the brunt of practical jokes and was pinched when leaning over a car. She found condoms and pornographic pictures in her tool box. "When interviewed, she was considering changing to a training program with more female students. Incidents such as these are common occurrences to young women in educational programs considered nontraditional for their sex," Stein said. "Although young men can also be victims of sexual harassment, it occurs less frequently, is usually less severe in form and seems to have less impact on their self-esteem and life choices."[23]

One study found that 65 percent of girls reported harassment by male classmates and some teachers in nontraditional high school classes.[24]

## Is Any Notice by Peers Better than None?

Popularity is a crazy game. Sometimes, getting noticed in an inappropriate way might seem to be better than feeling invisible.

Females are not just targets of sexual harassment; sometimes they are the harassers.

Some children will misbehave for attention. Negative attention, being scolded or punished, is sometimes preferable to no attention at all.

Do not confuse sexual harassment for attention. Do not allow others to treat you in a way that makes you uncomfortable. Do not convince yourself that it is better than not being noticed.

The identity of the victim of sexual harassment is not important. You are not getting the kind of attention you might think you are getting. You are merely at the right place at the right time. The words, looks, and gestures are being thrown at a moving target. Your identity is not important, so the "attention" is empty.

Nothing about sexual harassment is positive. Negative attention will make you think less of yourself; it will not make you look better in anyone else's eyes. In short, do not allow yourself to be sexually harassed. Do something about it.

## Why Are Girls Historically the Targets?

*St. Thomas Aquinas insisted that every woman was a birth defect, an imperfect male, conceived because her father was ill, weakened, or in a state of sin at the time of her conception.*[25]

*Several historians decided that Queen Elizabeth I (1533–1603) was too clever to be female. They claimed that she died in infancy and a boy was secretly raised in her place.*[26]

*A learned woman was presented as a curiosity to King James I. He was told she was fluent in Latin, Greek, and Hebrew. His only question was, "But can she spin?"*[27]

*In the early history of this country, women aboard the Mayflower were not allowed to sign the Mayflower Compact, which gave all free men the power to make laws for the new settlement. Women were represented by their husbands or fathers.*[28]

*In the case of* Bradwell *v.* Illinois *in 1872, the U.S. Supreme Court upheld the Illinois Supreme Court's refusal to allow women to practice law. Justice Bradley wrote in his concurring opinion, "Man is or should be woman's protector and defender . . . the natural and proper timidity and delicacy which belong to the female sex evidently unfits it for many of the occupations of civil life . . . the paramount destiny and mission of women are to fulfill the noble and benign offices of wife and mother."*[29]

*Theorists in the late nineteenth century believed that too much education was bad for women's health. The American Association of University Women commissioned its first national study in 1885 "to dispel the commonly accepted myth that higher education was harmful to a woman's health."*[30]

♦ ♦ ♦

*In* Muller *v.* Oregon *(1908), the U.S. Supreme Court upheld the constitutionality of a state law that prohibited employment of women for more than ten hours a day in factories or laundries. The court, emphasizing the physical differences between women and men, stated "history discloses the fact that woman has always been dependent upon man."*[31]

*In the case of* State *v.* Hall *in 1966, a Mississippi court upheld a state statute that excluded women from serving on juries. The court said women should be excluded so "they may continue their service as mothers, wives, and homemakers, and so to protect them from the filth, obscenity, and obnoxious atmosphere that so often pervades a courtroom during a jury trial."*[32]

*In 1993, in a sixth-grade classroom in upstate New York, Eve Bruneau finished with her work and asked her teacher what she could do. He said, "Why don't you recycle?" He suggested that she collect and organize classroom wastepaper for pickup. A boy asked the same question and the teacher suggested that he build a rocket. Eve did not want to recycle; she wanted to build a rocket, but was denied the opportunity because she was a girl.*[33]

According to researchers, girls' self-esteem drops as they go through school even though they do as well as boys on many standardized tests and get better grades.[34]

In a national study, 60 percent of girls in elementary school reported, "I am happy the way I am." That figure dropped to 29 percent when they reached high school.[35]

The traditional teaching of history in schools that recognized an exclusively white male curriculum and ignored the contributions others have made to society has undergone changes in recent years; however, many of the contributions of peoples other than white males have been given only token representation.

"Lowered self-esteem is a perfectly reasonable conclusion if one has been subtly instructed that what people like oneself have done in the world has not been important and is not worth studying," historian Linda Kerber said.[36]

A five-year study of one hundred girls between seven and eighteen at an Ohio private girls' school showed stalled psychological development at the age of eleven or twelve, even though they did well academically and had mothers with careers as role models. "The girls began to repress emotions and opinions; they grew confused and uncertain, unable to speak their minds, and they were paralyzed at the thought of even minor conflict," the study found.[37]

Interviews revealed the girls had learned from mothers and female teachers "that a 'good girl' attempts to please everyone, is too nice to express anger or cause conflict, politely lets the other person have the upper hand and thoughtfully puts her own needs last."

Lyn Mikel Brown of Colby College, co-author of the study, said:

> The very behaviors adults praise in girls—
> compliance, selflessness, silence—are the same

behaviors that are going to drop them out of the competition in the work force. . . . Virtually all the qualities needed to thrive in life—strength, courage, independence—also happen to be the stereotypic "male" attributes.[38]

Other studies indicate that teachers give more precise comments—praise, acceptance, remediation (help with special problems), and criticism—to boys than to girls in terms of both scholarship and conduct.

Some researchers say this is one cause of what they call "learned helplessness" that they see in girls. Learned helplessness "refers to a lack of perseverance, a debilitating loss of self-confidence. . . . While girls are more likely to attribute their success to luck, boys are more likely to attribute their success to ability."[39]

Although messages of worth are confused at best, as far as academic excellence is concerned, there is a crystal-clear message to young girls on physical attractiveness and sexuality. "Girls are learning that they are second-class citizens, only valued for their physical attributes," Sharon Schuster, president of the American Association of University Women, said.[40] The message everywhere is not only that a girl's value is based on her physical attractiveness, but also that it is OK for female physical attractiveness to be exploited. Look at the way beer, cars, or perfume (just to name a few) are advertised on television and in the print media.

A 1990 University of Dayton study of sitcoms on ABC, CBS, NBC, and Fox found that 40 percent of the sexual behavior observed was sexual harassment. "Lewd remarks, suggestive touching and other forms of sexual harassment are routine. . . . More important, it is presented in such a way to make it seem acceptable."[41] There were no consequences for the characters who harassed. "Male characters initiated 68 percent of the incidents, women 32 percent."[42]

Society gives power to males: formal power from positions of authority—principals, teachers, or employers—and informal power because our culture views women as second-class citizens.[43] According to Boston University professor Frances Grossman:

> From the guys who work on the street to the biology professor who tells a sexist joke in class, to the guy who says, "Hey baby, let's go out," to the guy who rapes—all these are part of a piece in their role of disempowering women. Men say these are not related behaviors. Flirting and jokes are fine, and rape is bad, they say. But increasingly, sociologists say they all send the same disempower-message to women.[44]

Part of a young boy's education and socialization is the idea that man is the protector of woman. We teach our male children the idea that power over women is a basic right and responsibility of manhood. Whether we intend it or not, our society teaches our sons that lack of power over women makes them less of a man.[45]

Boys are also taught that they belong to the superior sex. Strong-willed girls run the risk of having their spirits broken if they challenge sex-role stereotyping. There are many more "can't or shouldn't" ideas for girls than there are for boys.[46]

Even our language reflects the fact that females have less value than males. There is an old saying: "Tell me a people's language, and I'll tell you the values of that people."[47] Not only does language reflect the society, it shapes it. "A young woman who has grown up hearing the word 'policeman' does not consider that she herself might become one. . . . When she was growing up, these words reflected society; there were few or no women in these fields. But these words did more than reflect society; they shaped it. Many young women like this one based career decisions on the language, which said: Do not apply here."[48]

Inclusive language includes everyone; exclusive language does not. "All students should bring their books to the library" is an inclusive sentence. It means everyone. It says everyone.

"Each student should bring his book to the library" is exclusive. We know that the sentence "means" both boys and girls, but it is not clear because it says just boys should bring their books to the library.

Nonsexist language treats everyone equally. There is an easy test to see whether a statement is sexist. Just reverse the roles. If you can substitute a female for a male, or vice versa, and the statement does not sound ridiculous or wrong, it is probably fair to both genders.

Ask yourself: Could I write the same thing in the same way about a person of the opposite sex?[49] We hear terms like female physician, but not male physician; lady judge, but not male judge. Do not say lady lawyer, because you would not say gentleman lawyer. Do not write female artist, because you would not write male artist.

It is a common assumption that all explorers, pioneers, or settlers were male; that all business executives, supervisors, and officials are male. Avoid phrases like, "all the district managers and their wives."

District managers might have husbands. Watch out for constructions like, "Six people earn Academy Awards including three women." Women are people. Sexist language maintains and promotes attitudes that stereotype people according to gender. It assumes male is the norm, the significant gender.[50]

Females are historically the targets of sexual harassment because society historically has been male-dominated. As we continue to move toward gender equity, female victimization will decrease.

We have come a long way. But we are not there yet.

# 7

# Consequences

At school, Eve Bruneau, a sixth-grader, went to the bathroom to cry. She cried at home.[1] Jessica Hasenbank, a fifth-grader, cried herself to sleep at night.[2] Jonathan Harms, a third-grader, developed a tic, was inattentive, and could not follow instructions.[3] Katy Lyle, a sophomore, hated school and lost all self-esteem.[4] Tawnya Brawdy, a seventh-grader, made a will.[5]

Jane Doe, an eighth-grader, locked herself in her bedroom and refused to come out. She did not want to go to school or even leave the house. She felt as though God had forgotten her. "I didn't think that if He could feel all the pain I was going through, He would have kept me at Kenilworth [Junior High School]."[6]

These students are all victims of sexual harassment. Its consequences range from the inability to concentrate to failing grades, from hostility to complete withdrawal, from depression to suicide.

## Emotional Consequences

Students who have been sexually harassed report feeling embarrassed, self-conscious, less confident, and afraid. Some doubt whether they ever can have a happy romantic relationship. Some feel confused about who they are. Some feel less popular among their classmates.[7]

To dodge harassment, some victims avoid certain activities. Some experience anger, humiliation and shame because of their inability to stop the harassment. Feelings of betrayal and stigmatization can cause isolation and withdrawal. A sense of helplessness, generated by abuse, is reinforced when those who do stand up and fight lose the battle.[8]

Often a victim of sexual harassment feels incapable of dealing with the situation; this may lead to a feeling of inadequacy which can spread to other areas of life.[9]

Sometimes a victim is isolated from friends by an unwillingness or inability to take the normal risks involved in developing healthy relationships.[10]

Sometimes a victim feels ill treatment was deserved because his or her efforts to stop the harassment were ignored or unsuccessful.[11]

The emotional toll can be long-lasting and increase the risk of problems later in life, researchers say. Girls report feeling ashamed, confused, and angry immediately following sexual harassment incidents, and for a long time afterward. Sexual harassment has lasting harmful effects.[12]

Malicious gossip, if sexual in nature, is sexual harassment. This, like other forms of sexual harassment, can generate harmful consequences for the victim.

## Behavioral Consequences

Students who have been sexually harassed limit their own behavior in a variety of ways. Most try to avoid the people who harassed them. Some stay away from particular places in the school or on the school grounds. Some change their seats in class. Some stop attending particular activities or sports. Some change their group of friends. Some change the way they come and go to school.[13]

All have limited their behavior because of the behavior of someone else.

## Educational Consequences

The effect of sexual harassment on the educational experience is significant. Some victims said they did not want to attend school. Some said they stayed home or cut class. Some did not want to participate in class as much as they had before the harassment. Some found it harder to pay attention in school. Some made a lower grade on a test or paper than they had prior to the harassment. Some made a lower grade in a class. Some found it hard to study. Some thought about changing schools, and a small percentage actually changed schools. Some doubted whether they had what it takes to graduate from high school.[14]

Even minor interruptions in a person's education can have significant, long-term effects. Limiting or interrupting a student's education drastically reduces her or his odds of succeeding later and violates the student's legal right to an equal education. The price is also high for the families. Some experience increased transportation expenses when the student changes schools. Some families bear the costs of relocating to another part of town or to a new area in order for the victim to attend a different school. What hurts or disturbs one member of a family also hurts or disturbs the others.

## Physical and Psychological Consequences

Self-esteem is how one feels about himself or herself. Everyone around us affects our self-esteem: parents, classmates, teachers, and friends. The negative influences are as significant as the positive ones.

If a student attends a school where riding the bus or walking down the hall can result in insults and humiliation, his or her self-esteem will be significantly affected.[15]

Low self-esteem is associated with anxiety. Symptoms of anxiety include nervousness, loss of appetite, insomnia, headaches, and reduced task performance.[16] Headaches and ulcers are common physical complaints resulting from sexual harassment. More serious stress-related diseases can develop if the abuse is not stopped.[17] Victims often suffer from depression, and depression may lead to suicide attempts and suicide.[18]

Other possible responses are anger and hostility, which researchers have found can be linked to serious health problems. There also are indications that hostility affects the immune system.[19]

Sometimes victims experience various stages of

Sexual harassment is not restricted to the campus. It can happen going to or coming from school. This can result in the victim altering his or her route to school or dropping out entirely.

grieving much like those experienced after the death of a loved one. The intensity of each stage depends on the severity of the harassment. The three stages of grieving are:

- Shock, denial, and fear: not showing emotions, refusing to acknowledge the incident happened, and fear of being alone.

- Anger: wanting revenge, reliving the incident, feelings of powerlessness, and loss of self-esteem.

- Resolution: integrating the incident into one's life, where the incident becomes less dominant.[20]

Another consequence of sexual harassment is that inappropriate behavior becomes expected behavior, happening with such regularity that it becomes commonplace. Girls expect to be treated in an inappropriate manner and, though they do not think of themselves as victims, their self-esteem is slowly worn away.[21]

The physical and psychological consequences of sexual harassment can be significant and far-reaching. It can affect learning, which can limit career options and economic potential. It can also affect one's physical well-being, causing severe trauma or post-traumatic stress syndrome.[22] As a result of sexual harassment, people spend years in therapy in an attempt to get their lives back on track.

## Where Will It End?

The groundwork for how we relate with people starts at a young age. Our parents, siblings, aunts, uncles, cousins, and grandparents all teach us what is acceptable. What is acceptable at Grandma Doris's house may not be acceptable at Aunt Alice's.

Some children attend preschools or day-care centers. The rules are again different and unique to those settings. This, too, is part of their socialization.

Most young children learn the rules. They prefer that mom and the day-care teacher be pleased with them. Some push the boundaries more than others, but most would rather get praise than criticism. So they learn the rules.

Children learn not only what is necessary to please the adults in their world, but also the rules relating to peers. These rules continue to change as children get older.

The way a six-year-old girl and boy communicate is different from the way they will communicate when they are eight years old, or thirteen, or eighteen. The differences are due not only to maturity and intelligence, but also to the different ways society teaches us that girls and boys should communicate. Society is not necessarily sending the right messages to girls and boys.

Anthropologist Margaret Mead linked sexual harassment to the socialization process of children. She believed adults were teaching boys to respond to girls in inappropriate ways.[23]

The media are also instrumental in socializing children. Television is a mirror of society. If the shows depict what we want to see, what we believe to be the reality, they are popular and stay on the air. If they do not, they are canceled. Even science fiction can push us only so far. There has to be a believability, a thread that ties it to what we know or we will not buy it.

Some people feel that television sends the message that little girls are not quite as important as little boys.

Although children's programs feature more female heroes on network television than ever, they are far outnumbered by male heroes, or lead characters.

This subtle message, received by boys and girls, tells little boys: "Do not expect girls to have those abilities; they cannot possibly be heroes. We must protect them." It tells little girls: "Do not try. Heroes are boys. Do not do it yourself; boys will do it for you."

Since it is easy for little boys to confuse protecting and bullying, some become bullies. Bullying is often a predecessor of sexual harassment.[24] If we have taught young boys—or implied to them—that they should grow up to be women's protectors, and that power over women will make them more "manly," it is easy to understand why some have difficulty accepting girls as equals.

It is also easy to understand why, as adults, some men have difficulty accepting women as their peers. As opportunities for women increase, men are asked to face one of the most difficult tasks of all—accepting women as their bosses.

People do not suddenly begin destructive behavior as adults. It is learned in homes and schools. To stop sexual harassment, we must teach children that it is not acceptable. It is not acceptable when they are children, and it is not acceptable when they become adults.[25]

Schools play an important role in the socialization process. Ignoring sexual harassment in our schools sends messages of privilege to boys and inequality to girls and affects how boys and girls will treat each other when they become adults.[26]

So what are these messages? Girls are openly told,

# Teens Who Have Sexually Harassed Someone at School

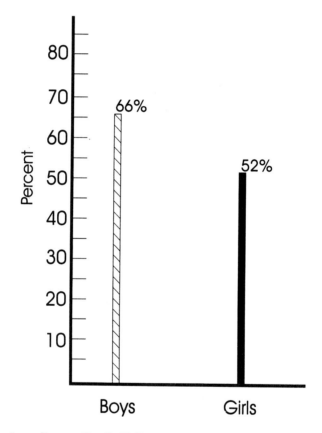

According to *Hostile Hallways*, two thirds of the boys and more than half of the girls surveyed said they had sexually harassed someone at school.

"You are equal and you can accomplish anything you want to." But there is an underlying message, which is fostered by allowing sexual harassment to run unchecked: "You are less important than boys. Boys have control." Meanwhile, boys are receiving the same message. Some learn how to take control and to adopt the superior position.

When girls act on the open message of equality—by asserting themselves, refusing to relinquish control, displaying intelligence or ability—they may bump square into boys who have gotten the message, "You are in charge; you are better than girls."

The potential for conflict is enormous. Boys may become confused when girls do not fit the expected pattern. Some might try to hold on to their superior position in various ways, one of the most destructive of which is sexual harassment. Girls are equally confused. When they are subjected to sexual harassment, they may lose confidence and self-esteem. They may feel powerless and secondary to boys.

The sexual revolution of the 1960s and 1970s destroyed the old rules of etiquette between the sexes and left adults at a loss to provide the social skills to replace them.[27] Before the sexual revolution, the roles for both men and women were well defined. Men were expected to hold doors open for women; women were expected to wait until the doors were opened for them. Men went to work to support their families; women stayed home to nurture the children.

After the social changes of the 1960s and 1970s, whoever reached the door first held it open for the other.

Some moms went to work, while some dads stayed home to take care of the kids.

Established norms no longer dictated what male or female roles should be. The negative side of this change was a degree of social confusion, but there was also a positive gain: the exciting prospect of not being limited by strict role definition. With equality came choices. Men and women, no longer restricted by what they were supposed to do, could choose to do whatever their talents and skills would allow them.

A new script for relationships needs to be written and young people can do it. If boys and girls are not taught that they are unequal, they will have no reason to believe it. If they do not believe it as children, they will not believe it as adults.

## False Accusations and Repercussions

Boys and girls are different. They experience the world differently; they communicate differently. Sociologist Deborah Tannen has said:

> Others talk to them differently and expect and accept different ways of talking from them. . . . Gender differences in ways of talking have been described by researchers observing children as young as three. . . . [B]oys and girls both want to get their way, but they tend to do so differently. Though social norms encourage boys to be openly competitive and girls to be openly cooperative, different situations and activities can result in different ways of behaving.[28]

If we understand these different ways of behaving

and the words used to accompany them, it will help us understand the different ways boys and girls view the world. Communication can be difficult between boys and girls because their viewpoints are different. Boys and girls misunderstand each other.

Often men view any form of friendly behavior from a woman as sexual interest. Because of that, men and boys sometimes respond inappropriately. What is meant as playfulness or flirtation by a girl can be perceived by a boy as something more. The boy may then respond in a manner surprising to the girl.

Kids are confused about their own sexuality. We expect boys to experiment with their behavior and girls to know what is welcome or unwelcome, appropriate or not appropriate. How, then, do girls let boys know when behavior is inappropriate?[29]

Sometimes confusion about sexuality and the difficulties of communication produce a situation in which sexual harassment is likely to occur.

There are several ways of getting the message across. If possible, tell the harasser, preferably with a friend or witness, that the behavior is unwanted. State what the problem is, how it makes you feel, and request that it be stopped. If that is not a possibility, write a letter. Again, state the problem, how you feel, and request that it be stopped. If the intent was not meant to be harmful, the harassment should stop.

A misunderstanding can be quickly corrected with little damage to anyone's reputation or feelings if notification is made early. Few people need to be involved, and those who are will quickly see that there has been a miscommunication. Repercussions should be minimal.

Repercussions from someone lying or making things up, however, are not minimal. When an adult has been falsely charged with sexual harassment, especially if that charge was brought by a minor, repercussions are often extreme. If the adult is a teacher or someone who works with children, the charge can be front-page news. Contrary to the way the legal system is designed to work, many people are quick to assume a person's guilt before guilt has been proven.

Accusing someone falsely is horrific, unjustifiable, and inexcusable. False accusations tend to blur the already difficult definitions of sexual harassment. They diminish the credibility of true victims of harassment and detract from serious investigations. Wielded for revenge, false accusations are a powerful weapon that can cause damage as serious as that of sexual harassment.

## Legislation, Cases, and Outcomes

The Civil Rights Act, Title VII, of 1964 prohibits sexual and racial discrimination at work. The Civil Rights Act, Title IX, of 1972 prohibits sexual and racial discrimination against students and staff in educational programs or activities that receive federal funds. It says students can sue to collect monetary damages from the school, and that the school can lose federal funds. The Civil Rights Act of 1991 says a victim of sexual harassment can sue an employer for compensatory and punitive damages.

The first sexual harassment cases to reach the courts were from the workplace. Then, institutions of higher education were taken to the courts. In recent years, elementary and secondary schools have been sued.

Here is a brief summary of some of the cases that helped define where we are today:

*1980,* Continental Can *v.* Minnesota: *The court ruled that an employer or organization was liable for sexual harassment and must take prompt action.*[30]

*1986,* Meritor Savings Bank *v.* Vinson: *The U.S. Supreme Court said sexual harassment was a form of sexual discrimination and that, in some cases, employers could be held responsible (whether they had knowledge of the harassment or not) if their supervisory personnel engage in harassment.*[31]

*1991,* Ellison *v.* Brady: *The Court ruled that a "reasonable woman" rather than a "reasonable person" standard applied in sexual harassment cases when a woman had been sexually harassed. The Court said:*

Many women share common concerns which men do not necessarily share. For example, because women are disproportionately victims of rape and sexual assault, women have a stronger incentive to be concerned with sexual behavior. Women who are victims of mild forms of sexual harassment may understandably worry whether a harasser's conduct is merely a prelude to violent sexual assault. Men,

85

who are rarely victims of sexual assault, may view sexual conduct in a vacuum without a full appreciation of the social setting of the underlying threat of violence that a woman may perceive.[32]

*1991,* Lyle *v.* #709 Independent School District: *This was one of the first peer-to-peer cases and the first suit filed against a high school in a sexual harassment case. The plaintiff argued that a school district is responsible for the actions of individual students, even when their identity is unknown.*[33]

*1992,* Brawdy *v.* Petaluma School District: *Filed in 1988 with the Department of Education Office of Civil Rights, this was the first peer-to-peer sexual harassment complaint filed with the Office of Civil Rights. Tawnya Brawdy, victim of name-calling, chanting, and gestures, settled out of court.*[34]

*1992,* Franklin *v.* Gwinnett County, Georgia, Public Schools: *The U.S. Supreme Court ruled that Christine Franklin had the right to seek monetary damages, in addition to other remedies, from schools and school officials. Before this case, it was thought that Title IX could only back a legal order to stop discriminatory practices.*[35]

*1993*, Harris *v.* Forklift Systems Inc.: *The U.S. Supreme Court decision returning the case to a lower court made it possible for people to win sexual harassment suits by showing the work environment to be hostile and abusive. The court ruled that the plaintiff did not have to prove psychological damage to prove harassment. Teresa Harris settled out of court.*[36]

◆ ◆ ◆

*1993*, Mutziger *v.* Eden Prairie School District: *This case was the first federal finding of sexual harassment at the elementary-school level. The U.S. Department of Education Office of Civil Rights ruled that Eden Prairie School District in Minnesota had violated Title IX of the Civil Rights Act of 1972 by allowing the sexual harassment of second-grader Cheltzie Hentz and seven other elementary and junior high school girls. (The claim was filed by Cheltzie's mother, Sue Mutziger.)*[37]

◆ ◆ ◆

*1993*, Jane Doe *v.* Petaluma School District: *This was the first one-million-dollar lawsuit filed claiming sexual harassment from classmates.*[38]

◆ ◆ ◆

# 8

## What Can You Do When You Are Sexually Harassed?

You are being sexually harassed. You do not want to believe it. You just want it to all go away. You want your old life back. You want to wake up and have the bad dream stop. But you are awake, and your life has changed.

The first thing to do is talk to someone. Tell them what is happening to you. Be specific. Give details. Do not keep it a secret. Do not ignore it. By sharing the experience, you will be validating it and you will be on the way to stopping it. By keeping it a secret, you can only hope that it will stop on its own—most likely it will not. Talk to your friends. Have they had similar experiences? You are probably not the only victim. You may take group action if others are involved: Talk to a teacher or counselor together.

If it is only happening to you, or you cannot share it

# Answer These Questions When Reporting Sexual Harassment

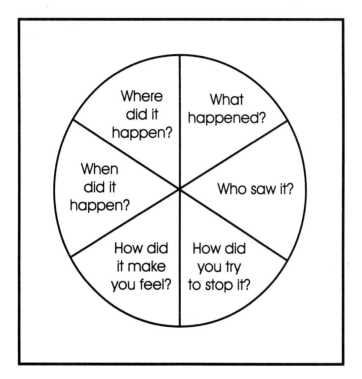

When reporting sexual harassment, be specific. Information should be as detailed as possible.

with a friend or relative, talk to a teacher or counselor at school. If that will not work, go to a professional counselor. Do not keep it to yourself. Doing nothing only increases the feeling of helplessness.

Do not blame yourself. It is not your fault that someone is harassing you. It is an action someone else chose to take. Do not play mind games with yourself trying to figure out what you did wrong to bring this on so you can change and fix it. You did not do anything wrong. You do not deserve to be harassed.

Do not wait. By waiting, you only enable it to continue. If you decide to file charges, and you put it off, you might miss the time limit for filing.[1] Because the time limit for filing a complaint varies from state to state, contact the Civil Rights Commission at your state capital.

## How Do You Stop Sexual Harassment Directed Toward You?

Try to evaluate your situation. Sometimes telling the person to stop works. Sometimes threatening to tell a teacher or parent works. Sometimes neither of these approaches is a possibility. Share the situation with someone you trust. Get another opinion.[2]

The decision must be yours. It must be something that you are comfortable doing. If you are not comfortable talking to the person harassing you, do not do it. If it seems like a reasonable thing to do, try it.

Keep in mind, it is possible that the person harassing you does not realize that what he or she is doing is unwanted. If that is the case, and you inform this person that it is not an appropriate way to communicate with you, it could stop.

90

Sometimes inappropriate behavior is a failed attempt to make someone notice. Sometimes the harasser is not trying to put the victim down, but instead is trying to attract the person's attention. The harasser might think the behavior is funny and be confused when the object of his or her attention becomes angry. The harasser may not realize how much it is hurting the victim. Maybe the harasser thinks it is cool and would be surprised that some students disapprove of the action. If the harasser feels backed into a corner, he or she might not know how to stop the behavior without looking foolish.[3]

Girls "find their harassers disgusting—not, as some harassers mistakenly believe, sexually attractive. . . . Boys are often amazed to learn that their behavior is seen as a turn-off by girls," said Susan Strauss, author of *Sexual Harassment and Teens.*[4]

See whether a group setting can be arranged with a teacher or counselor where girls can express their discomfort to boys in a discussion forum and make them aware that some behavior boys think is playful is not seen that way by girls.

It is important to remember that girls and boys often view situations very differently. This does not excuse sexual harassment, but it can sometimes explain inappropriate behavior.

If someone repeatedly asks you out, and you repeatedly turn the person down by making an excuse rather than saying that you are not interested, you are sending mixed messages. Do not waffle. Do not be evasive. Be firm, direct, and honest, but do not forget to consider the person's feelings.

If you are confronting someone who has been

sexually harassing you, make sure there is no room for misinterpretation. If you have made the decision to talk to the person, do not confuse the situation by being evasive. Be straightforward, direct, and honest. Tell them specifically that their behavior is inappropriate and that you do not like it. Then tell them to stop.

If you have tried to communicate your feelings with the harasser and the harassment has not stopped or if you cannot talk to the harasser, try writing a letter. The letter should clearly state three things: what the problem is (what happened, when, where, and how often); how the behavior made you feel; and a request that the behavior stop.[5]

The letter can also state your options if the harassment does not stop. It should be specific. The assistance of a parent or a counselor might be helpful to assure simplicity and accuracy. Document incidents and collect evidence if possible. Save a copy of the letter in case you need it in the future.

In addition to the possibility that the letter might solve the problem, it also could be therapeutic, a silent form of intervention. Such action may help a victim feel less helpless.[6]

There are some who do not advocate the letter approach. They argue that it puts too much responsibility on the victim, that it is not the victim's obligation to take action to right a wrong that he or she did not cause. Linda Purrington, editor of *Parents for Title IX Newsletter*, said:

> This approach •Makes the child responsible for dealing with the situation, whereas it is the adults who are responsible for changing the school environment. •Presumes that the victim can

communicate from a position of power. . . . •Presumes (falsely) that telling the harasser something is unwelcome makes any difference at all to the harasser.[7]

This is a valid argument. Victims must decide for themselves the best course of action. What is right for one person is not necessarily right for another.

If your choice is to write a letter or talk with the harasser, do not put yourself in a dangerous situation. Be smart. Avoid confrontation if it would put you in a compromising situation. Avoid isolated areas. Pay attention to your instincts.[8]

## When Does Sexual Harassment Warrant Asking for Help?

In the following situations, it is extremely important that you ask for help and not deal with the problem on your own:

- If the harasser tries to make you promise to keep the harassment a secret.
- If the offender is an adult.
- If the harassment happens only when you are alone with the person.
- If you are physically hurt or threatened.[9]

## What Do You Do If You Cannot Go to Parents or Teachers or If Your Concerns Are Not Taken Seriously?

Friends are great, but they can only do so much. The time comes when adult intervention is necessary. If you cannot go to your parents or teachers, or you have discussed it with them and they either are not taking you seriously or are not taking appropriate action, you must

Students can be sexually harassed by teachers, administrators, and other school personnel. If an adult requests sexual favors from you, it is important that you ask someone you trust for help.

reach out to someone else. Think about other relatives who might be helpful, or maybe a friend has parents you can talk to.

Check the student handbook. See whether your school has a policy against sexual harassment. It might state students' rights and responsibilities. Some schools appoint a complaint manager. Find out how your school handles complaints or helps prevent sexual harassment.

Look for the names of women's organizations in your community. Check for a local chapter of the National Organization for Women or the American Association of University Women. If you have a university or college in your area, call the Women's Studies Department and ask for the names of organizations that might help.

Check the newspaper. Many run listings of organizations and their phone numbers. Some have a representative who could provide the information. The newspaper's library staff might also be able to get the information.

Call the Department of Education in your state, the Equal Employment Opportunity Commission, or the U.S. Department of Education Office for Civil Rights.

## What About Legal Action?

Legal action may be appropriate, but it should be considered after all other avenues have been explored. Legal action can be expensive, stressful, and time-consuming. It should be initiated only after a formal complaint has been filed with the school or organization and the outcome is not satisfactory.

If your school is not adequately responding to your complaints, initiate a formal grievance action. If you are not satisfied with the outcome of the investigation, contact your state Office of Civil Rights, the U.S. Department of Education Office of Civil Rights, or a lawyer.[10]

If the decision has been made to take legal action, it is important that the accusations can be backed up. Witnesses or documentation of incidents is important. Formal notice should be given to the school or organization of intent to sue.

Gender discrimination laws vary from state to state. There are restrictions on how much time you have to file a claim following a charge of sexual harassment. Call the Civil Rights Commission in the state capital to find out what the laws are in your state. You can get the phone number from your public library.

If you decide to pursue legal action, be prepared both emotionally as well as financially; it is not easy to embark on a legal journey. Sometimes it is the only right thing to do.

The decision to sue is an extremely important one. For some, it means taking control, taking charge of their own lives, taking action, and moving forward. It is therapeutic for them and the only way to proceed for their mental well-being.

For others, it is a continuation of the nightmare their lives have become and an extension of the pain. It is the wrong choice for them.

Only the victims and their families can make the decision. No one should try to influence another. Others can supply facts, but they will not live with the decision every day of their lives.

Unfortunately, we live in a litigious (lawsuit-oriented) society. Sometimes the only way to effect change is to take the process through the courts. It is not a voyage for everyone, but we must thank those courageous enough to have made the journey; their efforts are in part responsible for the advantages we enjoy today.

# Chapter Notes

## Chapter 1

1. "Donahue," transcript #4109 (October 28, 1994).

2. Ibid.

3. Ibid.

4. Nina J. Easton, "The Law of the School Yard," *Los Angeles Times Magazine* (October 2, 1994), p. 24.

5. Susan Strauss with Pamela Espeland, *Sexual Harassment and Teens: A Program for Positive Change* (Minneapolis: Free Spirit Publishing, 1992), p. 3.

6. Elaine Landau, *Sexual Harassment* (New York: Walker and Company, 1993), pp. 43–44.

7. Easton, p. 22.

8. Ibid. p. 16.

9. National Public Radio, "All Things Considered," transcript #1520 (June 21, 1994).

10. "Donahue," transcript #3445 (April 14, 1992).

11. Easton, p. 18.

12. *How Schools Shortchange Girls: A Study of Major Findings on Girls and Education* (Washington, D.C.: American Association of University Women Educational Foundation and National Education Association, 1992), p. 38.

## Chapter 2

1. John M. Leighty, "When Teasing Goes Over the Line," *This World* (November 8, 1992), p. 14.

2. Ibid.

3. Nina J. Easton, "The Law of the School Yard," *Los Angeles Times Magazine* (October 2, 1994), p. 22.

4. David Ferrell, "Lakewood Students Defend Arrested Boys," *The Fresno Bee* (March 20, 1993), p. A3.

5. "Donahue," transcript #4109 (October 28, 1994).

6. Ibid.

7. Ibid.

8. Easton, p. 16.

9. Robert J. Shoop and Jack W. Hayhow, Jr., *Sexual Harassment in Our Schools* (Boston: Allyn and Bacon, 1994), p. 12.

10. Ibid. p. 13.

11. Ibid. p. 89.

12. Susan Strauss, "Sexual Harassment at an Early Age," *Principal* (September 1994), p. 28.

13. Shoop, p. 16.

14. Ibid. pp. 89–90.

15. Rosalie Maggio, *The Nonsexist Word Finder: A Dictionary of Gender-Free Usage* (Pheonix: Oryx Press, 1987), p. 165.

16. Virginia Sapiro, *Women in American Society: An Introduction to Women's Studies* (Mountain View, Calif.: Mayfield Publishing Company, 1994), p. 30.

17. Shoop, p. 194.

18. *Hostile Hallways: The AAUW Survey on Sexual Harassment in America's Schools* (Washington, D.C.: American Association of University Women Educational Foundation, 1993), p. 9.

19. Susan Strauss with Pamela Espeland, *Sexual Harassment and Teens: A Program for Positive Change* (Minneapolis: Free Spirit Publishing, 1992), p. 8.

20. Shoop, p. 88.

21. Ibid. pp. 161–162.

22. Barbra Morris, Jacquie Terpstra, Bob Croninger, and Eleanor Linn, *Tune in to Your Rights: A Guide for Teenagers About Turning Off Sexual Harassment* (Ann Arbor, Mich.: Regents of the University of Michigan, 1985), p. 8.

23. Ibid. p. 8.

## Chapter 3

1. Clarence L. VerSteeg, *American Spirit: A History of the United States* (Boston: Allyn and Bacon, 1985), p. 135.

2. Larry Stevens, *Susan B. Anthony: A Mini-Play* (Stockton, Calif.: Revelant Instructional Materials, 1975), pp. 6, 9, 11.

3. Betty Friedan, *The Feminine Mystique* (New York: Dell Publishing, 1983), p. 96.

4. Susan Sharp, Lynne Shaner, and Margaret Wagner, *Women Who Dare* (Petaluma, Calif.: Pomegranate Books, 1993).

5. Ibid.

6. Mary-Ellen Kulkin, *Her Way: Biographies of Women for Young People* (Chicago: American Library Association, 1976), pp. 253–254.

7. Ibid. pp. 312–313.

8. Ibid. p. 37.

9. Sharp, Shaner, and Wagner.

10. Ibid.

11. Ibid.

12. Ibid.

13. VerSteeg, p. 742.

14. Friedan, p. 392, Epilogue.

15. Rudolf Engelbarts, *Women in the United States Congress, 1917–1972* (Littleton, Colo.: Libraries Unlimited, 1974), pp. 134–139.

16. Deborah Anderluh, "Women Gained Vote But Not Equality," *The Sacramento Bee* (August 26, 1995), p. A1.

17. Susan Strauss with Pamela Espeland, *Sexual Harassment and Teens: A Program for Positive Change* (Minneapolis: Free Spirit Publishing, 1992), p. 6.

18. Shana Alexander, *State-by-State Guide to Women's Legal Rights* (Los Angeles: Wollstonecraft, 1975), pp. 221–222.

19. Robert J. Shoop and Jack W. Hayhow, Jr., *Sexual Harassment in Our Schools* (Boston: Allyn and Bacon, 1994), pp. 1–2.

20. Strauss, p. 6.

21. Ibid.

22. Shoop, p. 198.

## Chapter 4

1. Elaine Landau, *Sexual Harassment* (New York: Walker and Company, 1993), pp. 43–45.

2. *Hostile Hallways: The AAUW Survey on Sexual Harassment in America's Schools* (Washington, D.C.: American Association of University Women Educational Foundation, 1993), p. 11.

3. Ibid.

4. Ibid.

5. Stephen Buckley and Veronica T. Jennings, "Teen Clique Made Impression—One Way or the Other," *The Washington Post* (November 8, 1993), pp. D1, D5.

6. Robert J. Shoop and Jack W. Hayhow, Jr., *Sexual Harassment in Our Schools* (Boston: Allyn and Bacon, 1994), p. 103.

## Chapter 5

1. Michel Marriott, "A Menacing Ritual is Called Common in New York Pools," *The New York Times* (July 7, 1993), pp. A1, B2.

2. Barbra Morris, Jacquie Terpstra, Bob Croninger, and Eleanor Linn, *Tune in to Your Rights: A Guide for Teenagers about Turning Off Sexual Harassment* (Ann Arbor, Mich.: Regents of the University of Michigan, 1985), p. 14.

3. Robert J. Shoop and Jack W. Hayhow, Jr., *Sexual Harassment in Our Schools* (Boston: Allyn and Bacon, 1994), p. 96.

4. Morris, Terpstra, Croninger, and Linn, p. 14.

5. Ibid. p. 15.

6. Susan Strauss with Pamela Espeland, *Sexual Harassment and Teens: A Program for Positive Change* (Minneapolis: Free Spirit Publishing, 1992), p. 13.

7. "Donahue," transcript #4109 (October 28, 1994).

8. Strauss, pp. 13, 15.


## Chapter 6

1. David Ferrell, "Lakewood Students Defend Arrested Boys," *The Fresno Bee* (March 20, 1993), p. A3.

2. Associated Press, "Teens Accused of Rape Find an Audience," *The Sacramento Bee* (April 19, 1993), p. B2.

3. Associated Press, "Student Faces Sex-With-Minor Charge," *The Sacramento Bee* (June 9, 1993), p. B3.

4. Associated Press, "Sex-Points Penalty," *The Fresno Bee* (July 30, 1993), p. A4.

5. *Hostile Hallways: The AAUW Survey on Sexual Harassment in America's Schools* (Washington, D.C.: American Association of University Women Educational Foundation, 1993), p. 7.

6. Susan Strauss with Pamela Espeland, *Sexual Harassment and Teens: A Program for Positive Change* (Minneapolis: Free Spirit Publishing, 1992), pp. 8–9.

7. *How Schools Shortchange Girls: A Study of Major Findings on Girls and Education* (Washington, D.C.: American Association of University Women Educational Foundation and National Education Association, 1992), p. 73.

8. Ibid. p. 74.

9. *Hostile Hallways*, p. 23.

10. Del Stover, "The At-Risk Students Schools Continue to Ignore," *Education Digest* (May 1992), p. 36.

11. Nancie L. Katz, "Support Group Forms for Gay Teenagers It Counters Isolation in Atmosphere of Fear," *San Francisco Chronicle* (June 19, 1993), p. A9.

12. Ibid.

13. Ibid.

14. Ibid.

15. Kay Harvey, "Elders Calls Homophobia an Issue of Public Health," *The Fresno Bee* (September 24, 1994), p. A10.

16. Stover, pp. 36–37.

17. Ibid. p. 38.

18. Ibid. p. 39.

19. *How Schools Shortchange Girls*, p. 11.

20. Ibid. p. 49.

21. Ibid. p. 71.

22. Ibid. p. 28.

23. John M. Leighty, "When Teasing Goes Over the Line," *This World* (November 8, 1992), p. 14.

24. *How Schools Shortchange Girls*, p. 44.

25. Barbara G. Walker, *The Woman's Encyclopedia of Myths and Secrets* (San Francisco: Harper & Row, 1983), p. 921.

26. Ibid. p. 924.

27. Ibid.

28. David P. Currie and Joyce L. Stevos, *The Constitution* (Glenview, Ill.: Scott, Foresman and Company, 1991), p. 13.

29. Robert J. Shoop and Jack W. Hayhow, Jr., *Sexual Harassment in Our Schools* (Boston: Allyn and Bacon, 1994), p. 77.

30. *How Schools Shortchange Girls*, p. v.

31. Shana Alexander, *State-By-State Guide to Women's Legal Rights* (Los Angeles: Wollstonecraft, 1975), p. 158.

32. Shoop, p. 78.

33. "Donahue," transcript #4109 (October 28, 1994).

34. *How Schools Shortchange Girls*, p. 67.

35. Ibid. p. 12.

36. Ibid. p. 67.

37. Joannie M. Schrof, "Dismantling the Gender Machine," *San Francisco Chronicle* (August 8, 1993), pp. TW13, Z5.

38. Ibid.

39. *How Schools Shortchange Girls*, pp. 69–70.

40. Jane Gross, "Sexual Harassment Issue Finds New Arena at School/Duluth Case Sets Trend in Award to Girl," *Star Tribune* Minneapolis/St. Paul (March 11, 1992), p. A4.

41. "Sexual Harassment Thrives on TV," *The Fresno Bee* (December 28, 1994), p. F4.

42. Ibid.

43. Strauss, p. 17.

44. Elaine Landau, *Sexual Harassment* (New York: Walker and Company, 1993), p. 7.

45. Shoop, pp. 30, 32.

46. Ibid. p. 42.

47. Rosalie Maggio, *The Nonsexist Word Finder: A Dictionary of Gender-Free Usage* (Phoenix: Oryx Press, 1987), p. 199.

48. Ibid. p. 163.

49. Ibid. pp. 169–170.

50. Ibid. p. 165.

## Chapter 7

1. "Donahue," transcript #4109 (October 28, 1994).

2. Ibid.

3. Ibid.

4. "Donahue," transcript #3445 (April 14, 1992).

5. Nina J. Easton, "The Law of the School Yard," *Los Angeles Times Magazine* (October 2, 1994), p. 24.

6. Ibid. p. 22.

7. *Hostile Hallways: The AAUW Survey on Sexual Harassment in America's Schools* (Washington, D.C.: American Association of University Women Educational Foundation, 1993), pp. 16–17.

8. Robert J. Shoop and Jack W. Hayhow, Jr., *Sexual Harassment in Our Schools* (Boston: Allyn and Bacon, 1994), p. 56.

9. Ibid. p. 63.

10. Ibid.

11. Ibid.

12. Susan Strauss with Pamela Espeland, *Sexual Harassment and Teens: A Program for Positive Change* (Minneapolis: Free Spirit Publishing, 1992), p. 3.

13. *Hostile Hallways*, pp. 17–18.

14. Ibid. pp. 15–16.

15. Shoop, p. 65.

16. Ibid.

17. Ibid. p. 66.

18. Ibid.

19. Ibid.

20. Strauss, p. 13.

21. John M. Leighty, "When Teasing Goes Over the Line," *This World* (November 8, 1992), p. 14.

22. Ibid.

23. Shoop, p. 50.

24. Ibid. p. 155.

25. Ibid. Preface.

26. Jane Gross, "Sexual Harassment Issue Finds New Arena at School/Duluth Case Sets Trend in Award to Girl," *Star Tribune* Minneapolis/St. Paul (March 11, 1992), p. A4.

27. Easton, p. 24.

28. Deborah Tannen, *You Just Don't Understand: Women and Men in Conversation* (New York: William Morrow & Company, 1990), pp. 43–44, 46.

29. Easton, p. 24.

30. Strauss, p. 6.

31. Shoop, p. 194.

32. Ibid. p. 197.

33. Associated Press, "Settlement OK'd in Duluth School Graffiti Case," *Star Tribune* Minneapolis/St. Paul (September 29, 1991), p. B2.

34. Easton, p. 24.

35. Shoop, p. 198.

36. Associated Press, "Harassment Case Heard by High Court is Settled," *The New York Times* (February 10, 1995), p. A25.

37. Susan Strauss, "Sexual Harassment at an Early Age," *Principal* (September 1994), p. 27.

38. Easton, p. 18.

## Chapter 8

1. Robert J. Shoop and Jack W. Hayhow, Jr., *Sexual Harassment in Our Schools* (Boston: Allyn and Bacon, 1994), pp. 128–129.

2. Ibid. p. 127.

3. Barbra Morris, Jacquie Terpstra, Bob Croninger, and Eleanor Linn, *Tune in to Your Rights: A Guide for Teenagers About Turning Off Sexual Harassment* (Ann Arbor, Mich.: Regents of the University of Michigan, 1985), p. 9.

4. Susan Strauss with Pamela Espeland, *Sexual Harassment and Teens: A Program for Positive Change* (Minneapolis: Free Spirit Publishing, 1992), pp. 3–4.

5. Elizabeth Levitan Spaid, "When a Letter Can Stop Unwelcome Advances," *The Christian Science Monitor* (January 21, 1993), p. 3.

6. Elaine Landau, *Sexual Harassment* (New York: Walker and Company, 1993), p. 48.

7. Linda Purrington, "Don't Require Victims to Send Letters to Their Harassers," *Parents for Title IX Newsletter* (October 30, 1994), p. 1.

8. Landau, p. 66.

9. Morris, Terpstra, Croninger, and Linn, p. 11.

10. Shoop, p. 128.

# Glossary

**abridge**—To lesson or reduce rights.

**birth control**—Control of how many children a woman will have and when she will have them.

**bully**—A person who hurts, frightens, or oppresses those who are smaller or weaker.

**coerce**—To force or compel someone to do something.

**compensatory**—An appropriate and counterbalancing payment.

**constitutionality**—In accordance with the constitution of a nation.

**contraception**—The intentional prevention of fertilization of the human ovum by special devices or drugs.

**depression**—An emotional condition characterized by feelings of hopelessness and inadequacy.

**discrimination**—To show partiality or prejudice in the treatment of a person or a group of people.

**due process**—The course of legal proceedings established by the legal system to protect individual rights and liberties.

**equality**—State of being equal; having the same rights and privileges.

**equal protection**—A guarantee that the same rules of evidence, legal procedure, and rights will apply to all citizens.

**equity**—Anything that is fair, impartial, just.

**exploit**—Unethical use for one's own advantage or profit.

**favoritism**—The showing of more kindness, indulgence, or attention to some person or persons than to others.

**feminine**—Having qualities regarded as characteristic of women and girls.

**feminist**—One who believes in the principle that women should have political, economic, and social rights equal to those of men.

**flirt**—To toy, play, or show light interest or attention.

**gay**—Homosexual; sexual desire for those of the same sex.

**gender**—Society's definition of character traits and expected behaviors for women and men.

**harassment**—Annoying, intimidating, frightening, or threatening another person.

**heterosexual**—Sexual desire for those of a different sex.

**homosexual**—Sexual desire for those of the same sex.

**hostile environment**—Unwelcome sexual conduct that creates an intimidating or offensive environment.

**impact**—The power of an event or idea to produce changes or create feelings.

**injunction**—A writ granted by a court of equity whereby one is required to do or to refrain from doing a specified act.

**intent**—One's mental attitude—including purpose, will, and determination—at the time of doing an act.

**intercourse**—The sexual joining of two individuals.

**intervention**—Getting involved in events to bring about change.

**intimate**—Most private or personal.

**lesbian**—A homosexual female.

**liability**—An obligation or duty that one is bound by law to perform.

**liberation**—The action of seeking equal rights and status.

**litigation**—Legal contest by judicial process.

**manipulate**—To manage or control by shrewd use of influence.

**nontraditional**—Not conforming to tradition or convention.

**obscene**—Offensive to one's feelings, or to the prevailing notions of modesty or decency.

**precedent**—A court decision that becomes authority for a similar case that arises from the same or similar questions of law.

**privilege**—A right or immunity granted as a peculiar benefit, advantage, or favor.

**punitive damages**—Damages awarded in excess of normal compensation to the plaintiff to punish a defendant for a serious wrong.

**quid pro quo**—One thing in return for another; something for something.

**racist**—A person who asserts the superiority of one race over another.

**ratification**—Approval or confirmation.

**self-esteem**—Self-respect, belief in oneself.

**sex**—Biological status, male or female.

**sexism**—The economic exploitation and social domination of members of one sex by the other.

**sexist**—One who believes in the economic exploitation and social domination of members of one sex by the other.

**sexist language**—Language that promotes and maintains attitudes that stereotype people according to gender.

**sexual discrimination**—Discrimination based on gender.

**sexual harassment**—Unwelcome sexual advances, requests for sexual favors, and other verbal or physical conduct of a sexual nature.

**socialization**—The process of learning appropriate behavior for participation in a social group.

**stereotype**—Fixed or conventional thinking which does not allow for individuality.

**stigma**—Something that detracts from the character or reputation of a person.

**sue**—To seek justice or right by legal process.

**trauma**—A disordered state resulting from mental or emotional stress, or physical injury.

**validate**—To support, verify, or give approval to someone or something.

# Index